Blues: For All the Changes

Also by Nikki Giovanni

POETRY

Black Feeling, Black Talk/Black Judgement
Re: Creation
My House
The Women and the Men
Cotton Candy on a Rainy Day
Those Who Ride the Night Winds
The Selected Poems of Nikki Giovanni
Love Poems

PROSE

Gemini: An Extended Autobiographical Statement on My First Twenty-five Years of Being a Black Poet
A Dialogue: James Baldwin and Nikki Giovanni
A Poetic Equation: Conversations Between Nikki Giovanni and Margaret Walker
Sacred Cows . . . and Other Edibles
Racism 101

EDITED BY NIKKI GIOVANNI

Night Comes Softly: Anthology of Black Female Voices
Appalachian Elders: A Warm Hearth Sampler
Grand Mothers: A Multicultural Anthology of Poems, Reminiscences, and Short Stories about the Keepers of Our Traditions
Grand Fathers: Reminiscences, Poems, Recipes, and Photos of the Keepers of Our Traditions
Shimmy Shimmy Shimmy Like My Sister Kate

FOR CHILDREN

Spin a Soft Black Song
Vacation Time: Poems for Children
Knoxville, Tennessee
The Geni in the Jar
The Sun Is So Quiet
Ego-Tripping and Other Poems for Young Readers

Blues:
For All the Changes

n e w   p o e m s

■

NIKKI GIOVANNI

■

William Morrow and Company, Inc. / New York

Library of Congress Cataloging-in-Publication Data

Giovanni, Nikki.
    Blues : for all the changes : new poems / Nikki Giovanni.
      p. cm.
    ISBN 0-688-15698-3
    1. Afro-Americans—Poetry. I. Title.
PS3557.I55B68   1999
811'.54—dc21   98-50996
                                         CIP

Printed in the United States of America

First Edition

1 2 3 4 5 6 7 8 9 10

BOOK DESIGN BY JO ANNE METSCH

www.williammorrow.com

Dedication

It is probably more than fair to say that my father was a ferocious fighter who never ever liked to lose. He would, in fact, say "I won't play any game I never win at!" And I should add my sister, Gary, pretty much feels the same way. Mother is a deep in-fighter who will quietly whittle, some could even say gnaw, away until she either wins or gets good light. I think the fight is worth fighting and I enjoy the winning when I win but I also like the pretty shot, the daring raid, the wonderful turn of phrase that may sometimes cost me the point but was much more fun than playing either safe or to win. But this book is dedicated to both a ferocious fighter and a hard worker who will keep hanging in whether it's 0–40, 0–5 in the third set or just so gosh darn awfully plain that there is nothing that can be done. She will not spray spiders and mostly tries to shoo the flies outdoors. Together we have saved hurt robins and relocated little mice. She is a good neighbor to squirrels and turtles. She is Ginney. We fight the construction monsters together.

Contents

People think the blues is sad. They hear people moaning and such. That's not the blues. That's just somebody singing slow. . . . The blues is about truth-telling.

—ALBERTA HUNTER

flatted thirds and sevenths

◼

The Wrong Kitchen

Grandmother would sit me
between her legs
to scratch my dandruff
and unravel my plaits

We didn't know then
dandruff was a sign of nervousness
hives tough emotional decisions
things seen that were better
unseen

We thought love could cure
anything a doll here a favorite
caramel cake there

The arguments the slaps the chairs
banging against the wall
the pleas to please stop
would disappear under quilts aired
in fresh air
would be forgotten after Sunday School
teas and presentations for the Book Club

We didn't know then why I played
my radio all night
and why I kept a light burning

We thought back then it was my hair
that was nappy

So we—trying to make it all right—
straightened the wrong kitchen

Sound in Space

It's as if you've been invited to the White House and you know you are going to smile so you want your teeth to be bright and you brush and brush but because you have a partial plate you are mostly brushing your gums and quite naturally since you want to look fabulous and make the first lady green with envy because you have on your only designer suit and a blouse that if you were honest you actually can't afford but the girl in Saks was so nice and the girl who approved the charge heard the panic in your voice and she, after all, had never been invited to the White House and what's more probably never would be so she said: "Why, yes" I will approve this charge but do you think you might *want* to pay us something this month and you said: "Absolutely" because you do *want* to pay something it's just that Saks runs up against Nordstrom's and Neiman Marcus not to mention food and shelter so yes absolutely you *want* to but maybe you will and maybe you can't and that's what's so hard for people to understand . . . that distance between want and able, you know? and that's what we need to talk about

So, of course, I remember Lena Horne singing "Polka Dots and Moonbeams" and my grandmother being totally delighted with the RCA Victor TV and her saying to Grandpapa: "We better get Nikki up because Lena Horne is on TV" and me not quite knowing who Lena Horne was at that point though now recognizing that she is a great lady who has fought long and hard for Civil Rights who is also a lady of Delta Sigma Theta and who looks so fabulous in Gap jeans that all the world now wants to be eighty years old and look that good so The Gap was very smart to ask to photograph Lena in those jeans and who was very kind to me when I began my career and who has remained very kind but that is not the point of her being on TV when very few Black people were on television whether or not they were very talented and haven't we come a long way though quite naturally we have a bit of a way to go but my grandmother, you see, always said: **If you earn a dollar save a dime** and it's not that my grandfather in any way disagreed but he was more casual about needing and having so I'm sure it was Grandmother who saved for the RCA Victor TV and even at that I have to acknowledge that she was so intrigued with Nipper that even if it had done nothing more than show the dog responding to "His Master's Voice" Grandmother would have thought she had made a good purchase though the TV also brought us Lena Horne so Grandmother was a believer and so am I and that too is a bit off the point only because it was Billie Holiday who sang the definitive "I Wished on the Moon (for something I never knew)" and to hear her sing like even though because of dumb restrictive drug rules that punished some people for some drugs though not others for others she would never be on television which was a total loss to those of us who wished on the moon while observing strange fruits that travel light and we knew hearing that Holiday moan that the moon granted wishes so I started singing thinking if I could throw a note high enough and strong enough there would be the possibility that it would be heard somewhere in space and that is what I want to talk about here

Science teaches us that there is no sound in space and I think that's hogwash because if there is no sound in space how will all those wishes get up to the moon and anyone with an ounce of sense knows science fiction is much better than science fact because science fact tries to prove things like Thomas Jefferson wasn't diddling Sally Hemmings and everybody knows people diddle people all the time especially when they can't say no so yes there is sound in space and a large part of it says: **I love you** in a lot of different ways and when the language is unknown to the hearer other people say things like that is gibberish but love can never be gibberish . . . foolish for sure . . . silly you bet but the basis of all relationships is love which is then followed by trust and not the other way around because if trust was the basis there would be world peace and safe international travel but what I want to point out since it is always so important to do something useful is that you should, quite naturally, floss and nickels and dimes have a relationship with dollars and sense but not halves and quarters and machines that tell you deposit more money and Good Luck when it isn't luck that you need but better science which can explain how and why when all is said and done we are left with this density that forces us to recognize the Eagle Nebula is falling into itself and will one day be a planet though mostly we will not be around to see it and then there are those troublesome Black holes which are so totally fascinating though no one can exactly put their finger on what makes them so important and I am here to tell you I know: the density of a Black hole does not *prevent* light from escaping but rather that once light encounters the Black whole it finds such beauty and peace and comfort it no longer needs to search which is another word for love . . . and I do

Nothing Is Just

Nothing is just . . . a movie . . . a book . . . a song . . .
a piece of cake . . . a car . . . a close encounter with a construction worker . . .
a misunderstanding on a date . . .

Nothing is only . . . just out in a tennis match . . . just burned on the grill . . .
just in the mail . . . just to the bank too quickly . . . just a little too close to
the foul line to be a home run . . .

Nothing is simply . . . correctable . . . clearly an accident . . . human error . . .
worthy of an apology . . . ever your fault

A Real Pisser
(Though I Really Love This Car)

It's like your car won't start on the only day of the week you have to be on time and you're worried as always about your blood pressure and your glaucoma which is pressure building up in your eyes until your optic nerve can't take it anymore and you are blind or on the matter of your blood pressure your brain or your vein or your heart can't handle the flow and you stroke out only you . . . of course . . . don't die . . . not only because you would rather be dead you think but because of course you would not but because you know it's some sort of a test that you will now be crippled in your speech and most likely the way you walk and how you hold things and well geezolpete things have changed and you liked things the way they were when your car started and you got where you were going on time

But then when things go well you never really have a way of being happy let alone thankful so when your dog comes when you call her and your hot water is on after three people have showered and the oven didn't have a hot spot so the cake didn't overcook and the grill which isn't a smoker nonetheless smoked the steaks and eggplant which made you very happy because it is seldom enough that things do what you want them to do when they are designed to do them let alone when things do something that they aren't designed to do if you know what I mean that you actually contemplate how things would be if they didn't do what they were supposed to do let alone that little extra that makes you so thankful that you are alive and well on a day when things are going well that you well . . . actually take it for granted that things work when everything your whole life should have told you Always Check the Sale Date on Milk and always always always open the egg carton and even check the eggs themselves because the one day you don't

9

you will get broken eggs or out-of-date milk and then it's like your car won't start or your dog won't come when you call and you are not at all expecting this and it runs your pressures up

Because it is always a pleasure to get into your car which is eleven years old but only seventy-eight thousand miles and you haven't had a car payment for over eight years and you even decided to make a huge commitment to that particular car by purchasing a CD multi-player for it though quite prudently you did not change the speakers and you are always happy to get in and scoot around on the really wonderful black leather pillow your mother gave you for Christmas and look at the beautiful black leather ashtray Ginney gave you for your birthday and smile at the silly American flag that rides in the ashtray because Gary had the Fourth of July at her home and that was part of the decoration and punch up the Charlie Mingus you have all but worn thin because you really love "Good-bye Pork Pie Hat" and anytime you can hear good jazz and drive a smooth two-seater things should be all right but

Today the car won't start though the horn will blow and the lights turn on and if you were in a more cavalier mood you would turn on the CD and listen to Mingus followed by Johnny Hartman saying he Just Stopped By to Say Hello but it is against the rules to just sit in your car crying not because you are late since you have practically made a career of being late but because you are late on the one day of the week that you wanted to be on time and that is just a real pisser though I really love this car

A Rap for Lorraine

She's the North Star
an old oak tree
the duck pond water
that the wild birds seek

She's warm to the cold
shepherd to the fold
she made truth
both silver and gold

She's our own star
shining from afar
her life a beacon
of who we are

The Faith of a Mustard Seed
(In the Power of a Poem)

I really missed the second part of the revolution. From what I could read and what I could see, not to mention common sense, it seemed to me that the revolutionaries would eat with the people, dress as the people dressed, stay where the people stayed so I missed all of the image thing that fired so many imaginations. And I certainly missed the picky food thing people got into.

I understand and respect the Muslims. They have a religion that proscribes certain things. They not only don't eat pork and pork products they also pray several times a day, they produce and sell a newspaper, and in my time of knowing about The Nation of Islam, they ran fine restaurants and were in the process of building great temples. No. I didn't have a problem with Muslims because I am not Jewish either though kosher chicken and kosher hot dogs are one of humankind's great taste treats surely not to mention matzo ball soup, which I agree definitely does cure almost anything. I just missed the transition from coffee to tea; from Coca-Cola to bottled water; from chitterlings to quinoa.

What I liked about the first part of the revolution was the poems. We really can write. I liked the energy we put into finding that edge and honing it. I'm a tennis fan. I like to think in my better moments that had I been born twenty years later than I was I could have been a contender. I know Althea Gibson was the pioneer but not much came after her amazing runs at Wimbledon, France and the US Open. Not a whole lot has changed either I noted as I watched Spirlea bump into Venus Williams and everyone get upset with Venus' father while no one said diddly squat about the bump. But hey, that is not the point. The point is that a group of people who actually started out not knowing each other formed a team and not only sharpened their game but lifted it. We went to Championship form poetically speaking and even now if poetry were an Olympic event our team from the Mighty Sixties would be as outstanding as the Four Horsemen of France or the mighty run Australia made in the fifties. We are, in the words of the great Curtis Mayfield, A Winner.

Like Davis Cup things we all like to hear each other read. We were interested in how ideas were approached and attacked. We were shy and self-conscious. We were bold and bodacious. We were smart, though we largely led with our hearts. We were not three musketeers, we were not the gang who couldn't shoot straight, and we were not Quixotic though some of us tilted at the windmills of our minds. We were one without being together because we all had the same cause in our hearts: Freedom.

We suffered the same neglect our ancestors suffered. No one wanted to give us credit for our assault upon the assumptions and language of this country. We were brave and we did not back down when the heat was heaped on us. We made it through the rain. And kept our point of view.

I like us for that.

I like my generation for trying to hold these truths to be self-evident. I like us for using the weapons we had. I like us for holding on and even now we continue to share what we hope and know what we wish.

And if we just could have found a way to keep the barbecue warm, the chitterlings cleaned and frozen, the pork steaks pounded and the beer on ice we might have gone just that much further. But we have been holders of a healthier way of living and we have pushed people to rethink the priorities of how we conduct our lives. Of course, Black people are stressed more because of racism than salt; we stroke out more because of joblessness, homelessness, no credit, no cash, no way to get to tomorrow than the foods we eat and don't eat. We need the dead rich to pay their taxes, the live rich to pay their taxes, the present rich to pay their taxes, the future rich to pay their taxes. We need, still, a new system. But I like my generation for trying to change the old system, for questioning everything and for having the faith of a mustard seed in the power of a poem.

Visible Ink

In many respects Samson was a vain . . . if not actually silly . . . man . . .
certainly he knew the source of his great strength . . . though he mistakenly thought it was his hair . . . and not the God . . . who gave it to him

Achilles' strength was thought to be the water . . . he was dipped in . . .
not the faith of his mother . . . who took him to the river

Women count on their looks . . . adolescents their youth . . . yet we all
look for a champion . . . we all believe in some sort of magic . . . whether
it is the state lottery or a longshot at the races . . . we turn to some sort of
otherness . . . to change our luck

Superman fell in love . . . with Lois and was willing . . . to give up his
great powers for her . . . in order to marry Wallis Simpson, Edward . . .
gave up the throne of England . . . One wonders not if the right thing was
done . . . but if what was given . . . was worth what was taken . . . the very
nature of sacrifice says: There Is No Parity . . . One does what one must
in order to be a whole . . . complete . . . human

And then there is that cry . . . that cry of Samson who recognized his own
foolishness . . . that cry of Superman who finally realized he was . . . indeed . . . more than mortal man . . . and must face his destiny . . . we don't
know the last thoughts of Malcolm X . . . or Martin Luther King, Jr., we
can't know the deeper thought of the Brown family as they sent little
Linda off to school . . . we might guess that Emmett Till's mother wishes
she could take her boy back . . . as we might understand Afeni Shakur

begging her son: Honey, wake up and let's go home . . . The greatest heroes probably have no idea . . . how heroic they are

Most people think of heroes as saving children from flaming buildings or pulling housewives from automobile wrecks . . . But it is . . . indeed . . . heroic to pay one's bills at the end of the month . . . to go to church on Sundays and sing in the choir . . . to referee a softball game or teach some child how to make apple cobbler

The heroes of our time do the ordinary things that must be done . . . whether we are applauded or not . . . Most of us are good people . . . Most of us want to do the right things . . . We want to be loving to our families . . . caring for our elderly . . . wise for our young . . . We want to be a hero in our own eyes . . . We celebrate the true Champions of the 20th Century . . . because they went one step further

They willingly made a sacrifice of time . . . fortune . . . and in some cases their lives . . . to make life on the planet a more meaningful experience . . . That they are African American can come as no surprise . . . The African American has continually stepped up when the right . . . the good . . . the proper . . . needed to be counted

The Champions of the 20th Century have put their lives . . . their hopes . . . their best wishes . . . on the line so that future generations will sing the praises of our people . . . who continue to know . . . where the true strength comes from

And How Could I Live On
(for Betty Shabazz)

Live? How could I live on—knowing:::::::Oh sure I could hold on
Wait—worry—But I had to hear the sobs—I know what I must look like

Live? I did live on—when the bullets rained I fell—over the girls I
knew he was gone—I knew I had to change things

We were partners—you know—we thought as one—Sometimes he thought
it was all—him—why not::::I knew::::it was us

The changes—the acceptable changes—The work—The worry

But We Pulled Through

The people who used us—stole from us—tried to divide us from each
other

But we pulled through

We were at the plateau—not resting but catching our breaths—The
girls were doing all—right—a stumble here—and there—but all right

Then this—this mark that could not be erased—the mistake that could not be
corrected:::::::::I only wanted to Help her
                        Help cleanse her
                        Help tame   her hate
                                Her fears
that thing that ran in his family

I brought the boy home hoping trying yes praying scared I was too old too tired to make a difference but trying

We argued:::and we argued:::but this to me—I didn't feel like it

I wanted my crossword puzzle and late-night radio—I wanted peace

I felt him before I heard him::::::::Heard him before I saw him::::Called out MALCOLM don't do this to me

And he threw gasoline on me

MALCOLM don't do this to yourself:::::Stop Now

and he lit the match

MALCOLM I called MALCOLM MALCOLM

and he tossed it

How could I live on—like some thing out of Richard Wright's poem—like an object for people to come view—like a shadow of myself No I could survive but could not live on Knowing my grandbaby:::::named for a great man who loved me::::::wanted needed insisted upon My Death

I could not live on and wake up—from that nightmare

This Poem Hates

people lose their lives over things smaller than birds or over things sillier than a fire the fire department said should be put out but the developer will not and I after all am just one slightly overweight woman living with one slightly underweight woman and a small though very noisy dog so of course it is only honest of me to say yes I am afraid of Kracker's Pipe and Excavating Company and mostly because I believe R. Kneck Kracker is a bully which means he is a coward I am afraid he will incite some harm because he does not appear to have ever been told NO in the modern day and the fact that illegal burning is occurring and smoke is coming into all the homes but I am the one who calls the fire department and they say it must be put out but it is still burning and there is no permit but no one really cares about any of us little folk who only purchased a home with the thought of living in it and paying our taxes and growing our tomatoes and leaving our neighbors alone except for an occasional Hot enough for you and That was quite a rain last night and since we cannot afford to purchase our own politicians we get screwed and we probably always will

it's like you squeeze your eyes shut real tight because you really think it is important to get sleep and stay asleep so that you can wake up refreshed but you actually wake up as tired as when you lay down and then you think that maybe something is wrong with the whole damn thing and you can't exactly figure it out but you think it has something to do with crazy white folks who are once again killing Black people for sport for fun for whatever reason it is people kill people which is not passion or financial gain so you wish you could go to sleep but you can't but mostly what bothers you is that you begin to understand rage and a pure hatred and why people drive as crazy as they do and why people are as short-tempered as they are because you feel this oppressive stress that says no matter what you do it will be wrong and though I have absolutely no sympathy with any worker in any office who tells a man that though his wife has breast cancer and will die without an operation you don't actually think you will authorize this operation so when this man walks into the health provider's office and shoots everybody he can it is quite reasonable to me since no one listened to him when he was begging for his wife's life and maybe the operation wouldn't have mattered it's not as if he could wrap an operation up and take it home and play with it all it represented was a chance and that was denied him but still . . . sad as it is . . . there are people who ask the law to help and the law is very clear that it only helps those who have the money to purchase the necessary equipment so that the games can go on in style and that is a very discouraging feeling to know that all you are asking for is a level playing field and to recognize that the game is stacked against you so YES it does push you to an edge that as you peek over you know something is very wrong that no one listens to you no one ever knows you are standing there talking so the papers say the riot was rice or heat or a cop but the riot is all day everyday no one pays any attention to you and all you are asking for is a chance to present your side of the question it's like you understand that you just don't matter and this poem whines because a moan is far too sophisticated and a scream is far too rational so this poem whines and whimpers and is afraid and wishes things didn't always have to be like this.

This poem Hates

Not Just Truman's Baby
(On the 50th Anniversary of the
Official Desegregation of the U.S. Army)

It's not as if it were something new . . . this act of fifty years ago
It's not as if it were virgin territory . . . they may have just married but
they were sleeping together for years . . . and everybody knew it
It's not as if anyone had a right to try to be embarrassed or to say it
was wrong . . . because it was right and it made us all proud

The integration of the army was not Truman's baby . . . but it was
born on his watch

Starting where . . . back before even there was the rebellion . . . back
before there was the *Mayflower* . . . back when the Dutch man-of-war
scrolled up the James River with twenty Africans who were traded for
food there was the integration . . . Had the Africans known . . . could
they have only not believed . . . they would have joined the Indians . . .
and laid waste to the interlopers . . . but they were brave . . . and they
were believers . . . and they were loyal

Even then

Not from 1619 to this very day . . . have Black men and women
declined to serve . . . and honor a flag . . . a nation . . . an idea . . . that
still rebukes them

Not only have we come when called . . . we volunteered when we were
unwanted . . . From the Revolutionary War . . . to WWII . . . men and
women of color have served with distinction and pride

It's not as if Korea . . . were the first time we were needed . . . Peter
Salem and Peter Poor were the first men to give their lives for liberty
on Lexington's Green . . . and despite the British offer of freedom . . .
most Blacks fought with . . . spied for . . . killed with . . . the insurgent
Americans

Black Union soldiers fought so valiantly because capture was a slow
certain horrible death . . . being drawn and quartered by horse or by
jeep or by pickup truck . . . Black soldiers returning from America's
wars abroad were tarred and feathered . . . Black soldiers returning
from America's wars in uniform were castrated and lynched . . . Brave
Black soldiers had their medals of honor retracted and denied

So Truman passed a law not for Black people . . . we have always been
better than the country we served . . . but to tell the whites who
thought it more important to be white than united . . . that Black
people are an integral if not essential part of this nation . . . And we
are to be accepted . . . and honored . . . for the historic good wishes
and sacrifices we offered America . . . Not only fifty years ago

One More Boxcar
(for the Underground Railroad)

don't run . . . don't look up . . . keep on inching . . . like an old inchworm
. . . whistle a bit . . . under your breath . . . don't look scared . . . don't run
. . . don't look up . . . after all . . . a mile or a hundred . . . doesn't matter
. . . don't look up . . . don't run . . . can't go back . . . don't want to . . .
don't look up . . . can't go back . . . to being a slave . . . it ain't right . . . it
just ain't right . . . slow down now . . . don't run . . . don't look up . . . keep
on moving . . . yessir I believe I am a bit away . . . going over to mr.
henry's place . . . to get that mare . . . yessir it is a long way . . . if you had
a wagon . . . sir . . . I would sure ask for a ride . . . no sir they didn't give
me nothing . . . just say Calaban go over get that mare . . . and a mighty
good day for walking yessir . . . but I will take a ride . . . don't look nervous
. . . don't look scared . . . just stand still . . . just stand still . . . inch on
down like an old inchworm . . . night comes soon and you can run . . .
find the candle in the night . . . find the light . . . and disappear . . . find
the light and the old Ohio . . . find the light and find the freedom . . .
don't run now . . . don't look up . . . keep on inching . . . inching along
. . . the old conductor will make a stop . . . and you will ride that freedom
train . . . don't look up . . . don't look around . . . just keep inching the
ground will open . . . and you will board . . . that freedom train . . . keep
on inching . . . inching along . . . one more boxcar . . . inching along

Nobody Trusts Silence

The song of the birds the rustle of trees and the tap tap tap of water
The gurgle of streams on their way to a creek
The smile of mother to daughter
The crackle of coughs the thump of a heart
The whee of a sigh that goes prancing
The voice inside that asks for a ride
When the spirit wants to go dancing

Nobody trusts the silence
Not banks that take money Not stores selling honey

Like night and snow and caves and icebergs
and quilts and big fluffy towels
Like pies in ovens and hot rolls on Sunday
the quiet that silence allows

The elevators go up up up to some dumb mindless tune
Construction workers go glup glup glup
because the whistle blasts noon

Some people turn out the light at night
because they don't want to see
Other people turn their backs
on those of us in need
All of us mostly make lots of noise
To cover up the greed

Nobody trusts the silence
Not the banks that make money Not the folks who sell honey

the President's Penis

the President's Penis is not . . . should not . . . ought not be . . . subject
. . . to public scrutiny . . . no one should wonder if he is cut or not . . .
long or fat . . . curved or straight . . . does he have a little red mole on
the end . . . the President's Penis ought not be discussed . . . in polite or
impolite company . . . should not be considered by terrorists "Is this a
good time to bomb" . . . is not any of our business . . . the President's
Penis is not a car . . . should not be a plane . . . ought not be in control
. . . is just a part of the President . . . like his fingernails . . . or his hair
. . . or his teeth . . . just something that he has . . . that we know needs
servicing . . . but we don't care to watch . . . like him picking his nose
. . . or passing gas . . . or removing toe jam at the end of a long day . . .
the President is not a king . . . or the Prince of Wales . . . his sexual
adventures with live grown women . . . which may or may not be affairs
. . . are not affairs of state . . . the President's Penis . . . and its production
thereof . . . does not belong to that Delilah who treated it like a Tootsie
Roll then called Kenneth Starr to take a whiff . . . does not need a
resolution from the House to say what a stupid idea it was to let that
woman in or that Penis out . . . does not deserve the blame for the
republican coup in the making . . . even a dumb potbellied
motherfucker like R. Kneck Kracker knows the President's Penis is his
. . . to use as he sees fit . . . as silly as it all seems now . . . wake up
America . . . the sexual shock is hypocritical . . . but unsurprising . . . let's
clearly acknowledge the President's Penis by refusing to acknowledge
it's there

the Inaugural poem

it's like sugar in a porcelain bowl or maybe a piece of crystal or just some fragile beautiful thing holding something sweet or maybe even just a handful of salt which is not normally thought of as sweet but if you've ever had fried chicken or fried fish or even very thin sliced fried green tomatoes though we are not limited to fried things we can consider even good Irish oatmeal not to mention a side order of grits which you can hardly find any place and when you do it is that stuff they call "instant" which isn't all that quick but it is pretty terrible and can you believe some people don't even know the difference which brings us to why we are here today

it isn't often that the so-called leader of the so-called free world asked a self-called poet to celebrate the various callings that people call us to and no matter what some folks say about wasting time there just are some things you need to be ready for because if you get called all you can really do is bring yourself to the calling so I offer this poem for the president of the united states in the hopes that he is already ready since he will not have much time to learn on the job while even yet recognizing as JFK pointed out there is no school for presidents as there is no school for parenting though people keep doing things that make them parents just as voters keep doing things that make presidents so though we frequently do not know what we are doing and the people who vote for us know even less we hope the president will try to be a decent person while he is president and we hope there will be no more star-chambers because McCarthyism kills people not just hopes and dreams and Starrism has killed our spirit and if our spirit cannot live we the people cannot justify ourselves glacial waters have dirt on top but are blue as they melt and even bluer as they break off and some people say this is an optical illusion because blue is the only color not absorbed but I think blue is there because the earth and sky are one and the same and if they are we all have a bit of heaven and a bit of earth and one of the things we definitely know is that the exact same proportion of salt to water in the sea is as salt to water in the human blood so all we really know is that we are connected with everything and each other and sometimes you just have to hand it to God when you see a baby hummingbird drinking at the petunias or you see your okra plant being consumed by little black bugs and you say to yourself I ought to spray those things because they are attacking one of my favorite vegetables but then you say to yourself as a better part of yourself maybe it's not the best idea to strike at something which is only trying to do what I am trying to do which is live out the full measure of its life

and somehow through the laughter and the tears we all will live so let's put the weapons down and let's put the guns away and let's not strike back at people whom we have initially violated and let's see if for just a brief moment we can talk it over and let's think about the new world we are borning and while we recognize we cannot repay the Indians nor the Blacks nor make whole again the Browns nor the Yellows we do not still think we should allow the Whites to run roughshod over the rest of us and we have to say that affirmative action is good and right that equal pay is good and right that paying our taxes is good and right that women have a right to our bodies and that life decisions cannot always reside with those who can enforce their desires with physical strength so this is an Inaugural poem wishing this country and this president well with the hopes that this country and this president do equal good to this earth so that this world and that sun will bring a brighter possibility to us all

Just Jazz

Last summer I became a bird
plucked straw from the fields
plundered cotton from old chairs
to make a quiet nest

Fluttered in fountains
twittered when cats were near
dug Miles and 'Trane for sustenance
and Billie Holiday

No problem
No Sweat
Just Jazz

Stealing Home
(for Jack Robinson)

let's draw a portrait of Jackie Robinson no wait we can't draw a picture of a shadow of a spirit zipping by of man who hid himself

let's draw a picture of an oak tree one maybe three hundred feet tall and let's add a onceler who wants to make some money OK now watch the tree fall to be shattered from its roots to be cut up for dumb little things like night tables and one hundred percent pure oak lazy Susans just what the wife needs for her summer barbecue all leftover pieces can be used for toothpicks . . . especially if we polish the ends

wait now maybe that won't do maybe what we really want is a picture of a mahogany tree black tall as old as planet earth herself here when adam reneged on his responsibility to protect and defend eve here when adam thought he could lay it off on the snake here when adam didn't want to work with his hands and couldn't work with his mind and ended up reneging on his sons one of whom murdered the other and there is adam still not understanding what his responsibilities are but always looking for a darker reason why he is a venal weak man with jealousy and envy his only constant emotions though sometimes he will throw in hate just to give himself a reason to act and re/act to the wonder the trees bring when he lifts his eyes and the great mahogany tree which is as hard as a rock sends cooling breezes down and there is old ugly adam trying to find a way to cut the tree down to adam-size

OK OK that's hard to draw . . . let's just put some lines in a diamond shape and show the dust kicking up and show a black man sprinting around the bases so fast that the people with the ball don't know which base to throw it to because *BY GOLLY* that young man is stealing home and nobody steals home except those black men who think they can fly except those black men who find some kind of shadow from some very large trees but there are no trees on baseball diamonds so why can't we see him stealing home but . . . yes there it is mother mallie sister willa mae and lady rachel throwing cloaks of love over him making the players not see him there is the entire black community throwing love at him making the hate of others miss the mark no wonder he steals home he has a path lined with love and respect as well as wonder and opportunity

so let's draw a picture of love and hope and responsibilities with a man as tall as the oak as strong as mahogany as swift as the wind with a heart so big that one day it needed to fly and has to carry the man with it so let us show the winds swirling and the dust rising but the sun shining down and let us name this picture Jack Robinson and call it Stealing Home to the love he both earned and accepted

Opening Day or Hey! Start a Contest

So don't make a mistake . . . baseball is not fair . . . does not care about Blacks Browns Yellows Reds or Women . . . No it is not a national pastime either The Klan The White Knights The Skinheads The crazy fat lazy white boys who can't throw bat bunt or sacrifice fly are our national pastime but baseball is a way . . . when stupid things are not being said or done . . . to pass a lazy afternoon

So it's only natural that the NBA owners can't control their urge to pay Black men who can put a ball through a hoop multimillions of dollars would lock those players out so that they don't have to say No and lose the services of the players but they can collude and then say I would pay you more but the salary cap won't let me which is sort of like the missionaries telling the African women you must cover your breasts since the sight of your beauty excites me

And I really don't understand why Pete Sampras is considered so boring when all he has done is play the game without spitting on fans without kicking at the referee without grabbing his dick and flinging it at people and there are those who say Sampras is boring because they think tennis is a white sport and the young man is a bit too swarthy for them but whatever the reason Sampras is a great player and old ass Bud Collins ought to get a real job instead of hoping for the good old days when people had to pretend he knew what he was talking about

And none of this has to do with Opening Day because Opening Day doesn't mean anything anymore since no one knows who's on what team but for sure the teams that play in the World Series which is not a World Series but a North American series will have an Indian name despite the reality that Native Americans have repeatedly asked that they change the names of those teams but the team owners and some of their more stupid fans instead of their less stupid fans refuse to understand why the Native Americans may not want to be a mascot

I know I don't

I know I would have a fit if it was the Atlanta Niggers or the Los Angeles Cocksuckers or the Kansas City Canutes or the Chicago Pollacks or the Boston Bastards and we surely could go on but the Cleveland Indians are Indians because no Native American has asked the Unabomber for help in expressing dissatisfaction

So on Opening Day which used to be in Cincinnati but now everyone wants to be first and since it is so far north though Cincinnati is the Gateway to the South it quite naturally snows but people used to stay out there just because the Reds are the home team but now that Marge the Nazi Schott has control of the team all you see are empty seats and that is a shame too because Jackie Robinson gave his life thinking he could make things better if baseball were integrated and now we know that baseball follows America it does not lead so goody goody that Al Campanis is gone and Howard Cosell is gone and at least the white boys who are only there to talk realize that they need to watch what they say and someone needs to tell the tennis talkers that players have names because

it is a short distance from The Croat to The Swiss Miss to The Nigger
and no one wants that Grow up tennis you are an international game
and so is basketball and so is baseball so on opening day considering how
much money the game has why not get a baseball anthem and stop the
patriotic bull since no one is loyal to anything but the almighty dollar

Start a contest: we all will enter

A Counting Game

A flock of birds
A school of fishes
A colony of people
A dream of wishes

A failure of students
A hatred of pimples
A flash of resentments
A seduction of dimples

A motion of athletes
A greed of malls
A warmth of grandmothers
An insistence of calls

The things we all have to count and collect
The ways to make one out of ten

A handshake of grandpas
A comfort of aunts
A triumph of Black women

2 Word Poem

This poem Is 2 words long . . . to hear you count . . . Slavery is bad for
the neighborhood so the Civil War was fought not to maintain slavery
but to maintain states rights and if you think the only right the states were
after is the right to have slaves well then you just won the Publishers
Clearinghouse Award . . . There will never be an end to movies about
how bad Hitler is . . . there is one every year . . . sometimes a comedy most
times a tragedy . . . occasionally a romantic musical but always very clear
. . . who is definitely right and who is definitely wrong . . . and there are
no tears shed when the wrong is defeated . . . There will never be a *Gone
With the Wind*–type epic that shows some white northern family in pain
over the loss of land and income because of the unfair competition slavery
offers . . . and there has never been *Amistad* or not . . . a movie showing
the dignity and integrity of Africans and aside from *Roots* never a view of
slavery with the end to winning . . . even our cowboys lose . . . the only
Glory is death . . . and our criminals who started the numbers game . . .
who set up distribution systems for the cocaine that Cole Porter went up
to Harlem to write about . . . the men and women who created the sound
of emancipated America . . . JAZZ . . . are made to be buffoons . . . We
have a right to our competence and person . . . but this is a 2 word poem
and you can easily tell that because there were only a couple of thousand
men at the Million Man March and only a few hundred women at the
Million Woman gathering but there were a million cops out at the Black
Youth Rally in Harlem . . . and the million helicopters that the mayor
sent finally started a reaction to the brutality which is why there was a
gathering of youth in the first place but . . . hey . . . there were only a few
hundred people out originally so the million cops probably shot and beat

each other . . . and twelve million Indians can only kill one cavalryman . . . while one lone ranger wipes out a battalion and to hear you count that makes sense but I don't like the way you count . . .

This poem is 2 words long because Black people don't get paid for anything that we do . . . We slaved in the wilderness to clear it for farms and factories . . . We labored from the rice fields of South Carolina to the cotton fields of Mississippi . . . We fought each and every war this country has engaged in . . . We put our money in banks for the Great Depression to slurp up . . . We syncopated the work songs . . . We created the Spirituals . . . We rocked the blues . . . We scatted the jazz . . . We danced the Circle Dance . . . The Cakewalk . . . The Lindy . . . We Shimmy Shimmy Shimmied the Charleston . . . and we watched the white folks record our music . . . take our dance to the Great White Way . . . and then turn around and ask why couldn't we come up to their standards . . . We put our pennies together to create a numbers bank and the state comes along to outlaw our stock market while creating something called a State Lottery Pick Three Pick Four Cash Five day and night but when it was Black it was wrong and now that it's white it's . . . educational . . . and oh neighbors don't you just want to puke . . . but this poem is only 2 words long because Mark McGwire has a legal steroid and not a single death threat but Hank Aaron barely got a plaque and did I miss it or was he on the Wheaties box and what did his ball sell for . . . and Sammy Sosa's ball is in an unknown void since no one thought he could do it though do it he did but the IRS doesn't have an opinion on Sosa's ball since it's not worth McGwire's but if Sosa was on steroids and not McGwire they would ban him and take the record from him and write editorials about how unsportsmanlike Sosa is to take enhancement drugs but that's the way they look at everything . . . and it don't count for nothing . . .

This is a 2 word poem because everything we do is not enough . . . not enough housing . . . not enough health . . . not enough jobs . . . not enough money . . . not enough S.A.T. score . . . too much salt and not enough margarita and everybody said the president lied but if I slept with a strumpet like Monica Lewinsky I would lie too so I don't feel sorry for Bill Clinton . . . and I don't feel sorry for Lewinsky because anyone who would keep a dress with come on it has another kind of problem though I do wonder which end of the cigar was lit . . . I do . . . however . . . feel sorry for America . . . the new McCarthy has a forty-million-dollar budget to look up the dress and down the zipper of anyone he chooses . . . and this is a 2 word poem that says no matter what is in the report the person who really sucks is Mr. Starr and you can count . . . on that

Monday

Now there you are sitting in traffic waiting for a gap so you can scoot on out and be on your way to work and as you listen to the tick tick tick of your blinker warning the folks behind you that you are turning left you begin to notice that a lot of people more than you normally think of are turning right and shouting things at you and you being southern born and bred throw your hand up and smile and say hi neighbor which in reflection reminds you of your father who was always a hearty fellow well met early in the morning and of course while you are waving to your neighbors turning right you have missed the gap and it is easy to see that you won't be late because being late is not an option when you leave the house at seven fifteen but you are going to have to hustle and actually the hustle was a dance that went out with the disco era and you actually regret that

The Bee Gees did what a lot of silly white boys did they thought if they take enough drugs they will be able to sing Black which in the Bee Gees' case is sing high and I do like the Bee Gees and appreciate the imitation the disco sound created and though everybody wants to laugh at it and call it elevator music it wasn't when it started because it started as gay America's coming out anthem and while the regular man on top of woman man penetrating woman man going to sleep woman going to masturbate was used to hearing Black sounds and making it theirs and even now people come up to Johnny Mathis and say you are the reason I lost my cherry or something and even now half the children in America are because of the sexy sound of Ronald Isley and even now the old smoothies who think it was the sound of Frank Sinatra which it wasn't because the sound of Frank Sinatra is the sound of Billie Holiday and when even tone deaf right-wingers recognized that everyone would recognize that they started calling him old blue eyes as if anyone ever sat at a bar in the middle of the night drinking one for my baby and one more for the road called for another old blue eyes I mean hell no you call for "I'm a Fool to Want You" and if you can walk you go to the phone and drop a dime in to see is he still at home but no one does any of that anymore because we all have cell phones so you page your lover now and I don't have a clue what quarreling lovers listen to but disco was revolutionary not because folks were shaking their booty but because it was extremely important to look good and be cool and if the disco era had prevailed we would have won the war on poverty and schoolchildren would now be deconstructing *Dinner with Gershwin* cause it is very very true I want to get next to you but they don't have a clue as to what to do with a gay sound so they could either try to turn it off by beating up the gays but the band played on so they put the music in the elevators to make it irrelevant like they want to make Benny Goodman the king of Swing like they made Elvis fat then put him in Vegas like they stole rhythm and blues and call it rock like they hope you forget that jass was first a term for sex which is fun when you are young

So you sit in traffic and remind yourself that you are indeed an old woman because there was a time line of traffic or not when you would have found that edge and slipped your car seamlessly into it throwing up your hand in that manner of thanks while skipping off to work but today Charlie Mingus is playing "Slop" and you always thought the "Slop" was a dance your sister and her Indianapolis friends did to a tune called "Searchin' " by a group called the Coasters speaking of which there has been no traffic for the last five minutes so you need to hit it and get in traffic and go to work and be a productive citizen and work hard so that you can pay your taxes and eat your broccoli so that you will stay healthy and go to the mall so that other people can be productive citizens and do the right thing so that your family can be proud of you and the duct-work on your heat pump can be paid for and all manner of being responsible should fall on your shoulders and you should bravely brazenly boldly take up the cudgel but Thelonious Monk will be the next CD so you sit there waiting for the dissonance of harmony while your neighbors keep calling out good morning

Road Rage
(for ACUHO-1 1998)

the contract said you are to speak one hour and fifteen minutes . . . which actually . . . is no problem because you have the capacity to speak . . . nonstop . . . for days and days and days making you think you should have been . . . may have been . . . maybe even used to be . . . some sort of southern senator filibustering or a Texaco executive discussing policy or the republican relations person rehearsing Linda Tripp . . . but since you feel that time is a suggestion and not in any way shape or form an absolute . . . one hour and fifteen minutes is the outside not the envelope and you . . . after all . . . remember very well when Myrlie Evers-Williams came to speak at Rotary and asked: What do they mean one hour? and was told: In one hour everyone will walk out whether you are finished or not . . . so the one hour should be . . . or less . . . because no matter who you are and what you are saying the next session . . . meeting . . . thing . . . happens and everyone as at the tea party with the Mad Hatter and Tweedle Dee and Tweedle Dum will move down move down move down because things must run on time so if you should happen to be an artist who is brought not in chains but certainly in some reflection of a cage upupup the stairs of a stadium where an NCAA basketball team has done pretty well in the last decade so you know the arena is big but the group has cordoned off one-fourth of the stadium which shows you how very big and they have put a teeny tiny stage that should you step forward or backwards or sideways you will fall off and you being of the age falls frighten you stand very still and deliver your speech as best you can under frightening circumstances and then you say thank you and sit down and the head of the organization and the Black woman with gray in her hair who introduced you and the outgoing head all say we will not pay you because you were short on the time we have . . . after all a contract and

4 4

then it hits you . . . which you knew all along . . . that people who say how much they admire your work and how you helped get them and their people through difficult times don't give a damn that you were only doing the best you could under very bad circumstances what they care about is how much time you took up so that quality has no relationship to quantity and that's when you get a flash . . . ROAD RAGE

Now ROAD RAGE is not about the road at all or the pickup that is trying to run ahead of you because the sign said LEFT LANE ENDS 1000 FEET No . . . it is not about the driver who in a line of traffic runs out to the shoulder and flicks on his turn signal as if that is a sign that you must let him in . . . No . . . nor is it about the legally blind deaf man who if he lived in a civilized part of the nation (read East Coast) would have public transportation to carry him to complete his tasks instead of him having to take his and our lives in his hands because he or his wife or older brother who is a recovering stroke victim or he or his wife or younger sister is in need of chemotherapy or he or his wife or his next-door neighbor whom he considers old is in need of his medicine or groceries or bills to be paid or . . . well . . . something . . . and the legally blind deaf man is the only one who can take care of it and he is driving a 1985 Chevrolet that is actually in pretty good shape except that he is going 25 miles per hour and you are trying to get where you are going a bit faster than that . . . You may say . . . Whoa! why not just slow down and chill and get there safely but you and I know speed is not about being late but about rage . . . pure and simple rage . . . unless you are a teenager then it is about sex but that is a different discussion . . . the Road Rage we know is about having taken off work yesterday because the air-conditioner people said they would be there sometime between eight A.M. and five P.M. and when you asked . . . in a nice voice . . . could they maybe narrow it a bit they said why sure . . . eleven and four . . . so you stayed home but they never did come and when you called at five to ask why the fuck not they were upset that you cursed at them and they had no idea you were there their men got stuck on another call and it's not my fault that you missed a day of work . . . it's about the construction workers who are killing the birds and shaking your house who decided to burn their trash which if you could burn yours you would save a lot of money but you are not Kracker's Pipe and Excavating Company who works for R. Kneck Kracker so you cannot burn your trash and when you call the fire department on a non-emergency level to ask if there is a permit for the fire burning in the back of you and you point out that the last time they did that the fire burned for three days and you have had to keep your house closed up since May when they began destroying a field that you had been told was unfit for building the fire department came out and talked with the construction workers and you were standing in the street trying to understand why they can start fires without permits in the middle of the day and the firefool with the uniform asks the construction fools in the boots to please call in next time so that this run is not necessary and what is really happening is that no one is listening to you and no one cares about your concerns and you have no rights that anyone is bound to respect and you are finally made to realize that you are just a small colored woman trying to protect her home and that will not be allowed and while everyone treats you badly as they go about their destruction one thing is for sure they have to treat you equal on the road so you absolutely refuse to move for that eighteen-wheeler and you absolutely refuse to allow that other driver who is having an equally bad day to sprint in front of you and you absolutely do not care when you throw your coffee cup out the window and you are really daring some cop to stop you for littering when everywhere you look the earth is naked and alone and exposed like some cadaver awaiting an autopsy and someone wants to say something to you about one hour and fifteen minutes which indicates there was never an interest in what you are about or what you are trying to do but simply that you have been made to be some sort of prostitute to perform for some period of time so that satisfaction is guaranteed . . . and Bob and Bob say I have not done well by myself on this day at their thing . . . and there is a question mark here

I really do feel sorry for all of us because it is so easy for the big people to blast some rocks and the water in your well quits pumping or some group like Habitat for Humanity to purchase acreage that no one ever thought could be developed let alone would be and what was lovely about your existence has now become something ugly and crazy and if you protest they try to make you against poor people instead of against the idea that on seven acres of land there will now be 34 houses and the noise and traffic and garbage that go with it and the people who are saying well this is a good idea do not live next to 34 houses which sell for three thousand five hundred dollars while you paid eighty-five thousand and no one will take responsibility for the dry well and the loan you have to assume just to be able to drink water and brush your teeth and cook your food and no one takes responsibility for the quality of your life because the so-called good people are so busy doing good that the fact that your dreams are ruined means nothing and no one takes responsibility for destroying a wetlands because R. Kneck Kracker wants to make a little more money and the fact that you have to hire a lawyer to get him to stop diverting a stream onto your backyard and you have to hire a surveyor to keep him from digging up your backyard and you have to keep your house closed up and your air conditioning on which has run your bill up but no one is responsible for that either means that when you get in your car you already hate the boy holding the construction STOP sign and you run right up to him and if he doesn't move quickly he will be hurt because anyone in front of your car gets the brunt of everyone in front of your life and I do understand what is called road rage because it's not about the road it's about your dreams being destroyed a bit and a bit and a bit everyday and no one will even listen to what you are saying

Reading Lesson

C Delores run . . . run run run Delores

C Delores look pitiful . . . pitiful pitiful pitiful Delores

C Delores testify . . . Tupac did it Tupac did it Tupac did it

C Republicans give her the Clarence Thomas Award . . . take it take it
take it

C Delores see Tupac's death . . . wash your hands wash your hands
wash your hands

C Delores smile . . . never again never again never again

C Delores Tucker . . . fuck her fuck her fuck her

Truthtelling
(Sometimes a Poem Is All You Need)

I was sitting at my desk talking . . . on the phone concerning something inconsequential . . . when I noticed: **My** thighs were GrOwINg . . . It was the second time this week that it had happened . . . Was it the Pringles . . . I usually eat Lays . . . Was it the bread pudding . . . My sister had made poppy seed bread and . . . YES I had saved half for bread pudding . . . I kNoW better . . . I KnOw that drugs and steroids will swell the body when combined with food . . . **But** these were *little* poppy seeds . . . The eight million for $1.50 . . . Maybe it was my aTTiTude . . . Maybe I was thinking **fat** . . . I feared I could not be saved from a life of American guilt: **I am overweight** . . . Where is a poem when you really need one

Quite naturally . . . I said to myself . . . **Go exercise** . . . Go spend some EnErgy . . . Tote that intellectual barge . . . lift that emotional bale . . . Get a little giddy and you land in . . . the middle of a gaggle of poets Flying overhead. Laughing . . . not honking . . . at me . . . Flying V's and swooping wing tips . . . Showing the juveniles what must be learned . . . If mother goose can teach the young to fly . . . I thought . . . so can I . . . I huRRied back to my office . . . I knew the right PoEMs could be found

The redbirds always stand . . . out in winter . . . The little fINches stay around . . . but they are harder to see . . . THeir yellow coats are traded for a warm . . . er brown . . . But Mr. Redbird . . . all fluffy and fat protecting . . . Mrs. Redbird from peeping . . . tHoMaSines like me . . . sits in my River Birch watching . . . while she drinks and bathes . . . the slightest movement from me . . . will send them away . . . **Hey,** do they KnoW what it costs to have a fountain . . . run all winter . . . nOt one song for those of us whO spent our summer bUrying wires . . . luGGinG **concrete** and marble . . . making a haven . . . nOt one song . . . if I move . . . Oh! The eXasperation . . . the anguish . . . the simple desire to hear a soothing tone . . . There must be **a poem somewhere** for me . . . I hurry indOOrs

So . . . I pEEl four garlic gloves which I swish in a teaspoon of olive oil coating the bottom of a large heavy skillet . . . I brown the chuck roast on all four SideS . . . wHilE browning I cut up . . . not too small, not too chunky . . . celeryonionspotatoesandcarrots . . . Lifting the roast into the pot I add a bottle of rEal bEEr (no lIght . . . never a lIght) to the skillet drippings . . . Stir stir stir for about four minutes . . . ArrAnge it All in the pot. Place in the oven for two to thrEE hours (depending on what I have to do) . . . Go to my comPUTer to writE . . . I am now once again at home and content . . . But wait . . . My thIGhs are grOwing . . . Even as I sit at this comPUTEr . . . They spread . . . They wrinkle . . . They . . . **WHERE IS A POEM WHEN YOU REALLY NEED IT**

Be My Baby

I've got six tattoos—a real gold tooth
A shiny Black Beemer and that's the truth

My nails are long—my hair is smooth
All I need is you to groove

I'm too hot to trot—too old to jog
But the backseat is all right in Mama's hog

I'm yours for the taking I'm yours till the end
If you won't be my baby you can't be my friend

I've got chicken frying and a pot of greens
Cracklin corn bread and pinto beans

My best silverware and my prettiest plates
Warm peach cobbler and raspberry dates

I know what you say I know about her
Give her a call say: Keep the fur

Then come on home to me tonight
We can do the dirty and do it right

Somewhere Sometimes
(for the New York City Ballet)

Somewhere in that place we call space the universe is clashing bashing
banging ganging up on meteors falling up falling down making eagles
in the void dancing eagles rising tip toe jumping high jumping tall till
a new world can be found so they dance within that place we call
space
     somewhere

Sometimes in gravity's world eagles fly on Fridays scoping out a place to
perch stopping at jazz clubs stopping at fish fries resting on zoo branches
hiding from hunters taking their children to see the ballet in gravity's
world
     sometimes

me? I arabesquely stretch to reach the chow chow for the pig feet
me? I dégagé second plié relevé the Ajax to clean
me? I grand plié while still in place and watch me move
     through time and space
  I know I can dance I know I can dance I know I can dance
     but no one sees me

Someone in a city apartment or on a farm or in a small town where folk
go to church where folk go on hayrides where folks lean on fences and
gossip with neighbors while some dream of pizza and all-night skates
and some are wishing for hot prom dates some boys or girls are bending

and stretching and standing on toes that reach up to Saturn and grab-
bing a ring they hope to hold on to to lift them onstage where we all will
applaud

and they dance and they dance and they twitter and twirl and they
dance

for the New York City Ballet

I Can Sing
(with Regina Belle)

It's a rainy day and the robin who nested in the rain gutter at the corner of my house is trying to get her children to fly. One will not make it. She is on her side in my front yard. I don't know what to do for her. I can cry. I can wish her well. I can tell myself this is the proper order of things. We all cannot survive. I can listen to Regina Belle who sits on a cloud somewhere in the heavens drifting notes back to Earth in a smooth, easy manner like home-churned ice cream and hand-beaten fudge which, while it will not return that little bird to this form, makes me feel there is still a presence in the universe that sends a soothing sound when times are if not difficult,

> since perhaps
> had I not seen the mother clean an old nest,
> had I not watched her turn the eggs daily for two weeks,
> had I not smiled at the little heads as they chirped for food,
> had I not watched her urge them to fly

this would not be a difficult time for me, markedly unfair to little things that we love. I can listen to Regina Belle on a rainy afternoon when it is twenty degrees cooler than yesterday and remember some of the loves that are, indeed, worth crying about. I can listen to Regina Belle.

And I can sing along.

A Civil Rights Journey

Even when I was in high school, I couldn't understand why all the studies were of Black people. It seemed to me even then that someone ought to study white people since Black people weren't the ones who were lynching men and women, bombing churches, shooting people because they wanted to vote and I well remember the murder of Emmett Till, which I still think is the defining event of my generation. It didn't make sense to me that two or maybe three grown men could come in the middle of the night and take that young man from his grand-uncle's home and torture him to death. And then be found not guilty by an all-white jury. And then sell their story to *Life* magazine. And nothing was ever done. And yet people wanted to study Black people to see what was wrong with us and why white people didn't want to integrate with us. And I guess the real secret was that we didn't want to integrate with them but we did feel that public places should accommodate the public whether it was Woolworth's (which just—HOORAY—went out of business) to a public swimming pool to public schools. I remember all the arguments about your sister and I just loved James Baldwin's retort: It's not the white man's daughter that he's afraid I'll marry; it's his wife's daughter. And Baldwin was so cool that an entire generation wanted to be writers. Even then I knew there was something wrong with white people who would be as lowdown as many of them were. I keep wondering when will they go out and measure the heads of white folks and ask them questions about why they hate and why they murder but no one did and no one has and that's a shame.

The composer Andy Razaf wrote a song entitled "Black and Blue" in which he laments the color of his skin. "I'm white inside," the song says at one point and I still wonder what does that mean. Even white people don't want to be white inside. Even young white boys and girls listen to rap and before that rhythm and blues and before that blues and before that jazz because they needed something to soothe their souls. Why racism won't go away then has to be because someone benefits from it.

I know I don't. I know affirmative action is only right. I know that segregation was another word for affirmative action only when we reach out to white people we call it incentives when we reach out to people of color we call it welfare. When we want white people to change we offer them wonderful things; when we want people of color to change we increase the misery. Something is very wrong. When a nation will spend over $140,000 per cell to keep a man in prison paying out upwards of $38,000 per year because this person stole something or even sillier, sold or used some drugs then something is quite wrong. I use drugs legally. I had a lung operation that would have been impossible without drugs but I can't see the difference. My lung had a cancerous tumor that if it hadn't been removed would have killed me sooner rather than later. Some people are born to lives that eat at their spirit as cancer eats at the body. I'm glad I have hope. I'm glad I can read and reason. I'm glad I can take the time to have an overview of not only America but the Earth and now with Hubbell's Eye on the Universe I can speculate about creation itself. But a lot of people wake up in the morning on sidewalk grates, in city parks, in doorways of buildings, with no place to go that is safe and warm. A lot of people wake up in the morning and they cannot brush their teeth or comb their hair or wash their hands. They do not hear the burping of the coffee pot, they don't smell the toast. They do, I'm sure, feel the eyes turning away from them. They do know they are hated and feared. And surely they must wonder: How do I get through this day? Most of us have something to do. Even billionaires keep a schedule. Why do you think some people never quit working? Because work is defining; it tells you not only what skills you have acquired but also who you are. If work is good enough for Bill Gates it's good enough for the former soldier sleeping in our parks. Waiting for a gang of white boys to come along and make sport of beating him up.

So, certainly, things have changed. And there is a lot to do. The next century is right on us. Policemen need to give up their guns. Society needs to dismantle all our prisons. If we need to detain people a local jail should be sufficient. We need many more doctors; we need many more social workers; we need lots more teachers. And, yes, a lawyer or two to keep the stew honest. We need to be proud of the taxes we pay. We need to tax the wealthy dead at 100 percent. It's an abomination that the dead rich control "their" money while the living must suffer. We need a new definition of neighborhood, community, society. We need to make white America tell us why they hate and fear and hoard. We need a new definition of life so that we can find a truer definition of death. We all need a definition of responsibility. And I don't think there is any one key or any easy answer. There are some clearer answers and some difficult decisions but our first decision must be to change from the rather hateful, selfish species we are into something a bit better. I hope there are aliens out there and I hope they come to Earth. We need another perspective on the possibilities. Civil Rights have to somehow be tied to civilized humans. So that is the question: What is a civil human?

Train Rides

(for William Adkins and Darrell Lamont Bailey)

so on the first day of fall only not really because it's still early October
you sort of get the feeling that if you wear that linen blouse with that
white suit one more time someone from the fashion police will come
and put some sort of straitjacket on you or even worse CNN *Hard Copy
Politically Incorrect* will come film you and there you will be shamed
before the world caught in the wrong material after the right season has
passed and though you have long ago concluded that jail might make
sense for folk who drink and drive and jail certainly makes sense for folk
who beat their wives and children and there could be a good case that
jail would be significant to folk who write bad checks or don't pay their
bills you know for a fact not just in your heart that there is no excuse for
prison unless you just want to acknowledge that building anything at all
is good for the economy but if that is the case why spend the money on
building prisons when a region a state a community won't spend the
money on building houses schools recreation centers retirement com-
plexes hospitals and for that matter shelters for hurt neglected and abused
animals so it's not just the building but actually what is being built though
you can't always tell that from watching roads go up since roads always
take so long to build by the time they are built they are obsolete and we
could have had a wonderful rail system if we hadn't been more interested
in Ferguson winning instead of Plessy and the entire system collapsed
under the weight of racism you are glad you do not go to jail but rather
are shamed or more accurately fear being shamed into proper dress but
on the first day of fall when you know it's time to break down the deck
and put the flowerpots away since you could not actually afford to pur-
chase all-weather flowerpots and when you gave it a second thought you
said to yourself I don't think I should throw this good soil away and you

now in order to save money are on your way to Lowe's where you will purchase a big thing with a top that fits and stupid you you never even remembered that you can't possibly carry the soil down so in order to save the soil that you can't afford to replace you now have to hire two young men to carry the aforementioned soil-loaded thing with the tight top down the stairs to place it under the porch only your dog has been scratching and barking and moaning and you fear no really you know that little mother mouse is back and last year it was quite a dilemma for you since mother mouse started coming to the inside deck and you and the dog kept seeing these little nuts and of course those mouse droppings and you were actually going to kill her but your nose was running so you went to the tissue box and the tissue was all chewed up so you lifted the box and there clearly was something in it and to be very honest you were scared because no matter what we say human beings don't do well with other life-forms but something made you peer down into the box and there were two bright eyes looking back and you really expected her to run only she didn't and then you realized it was because of the babies which you more sensed than saw and even though you have to admit to yourself you are afraid you take the box and place it in a hollow log in the meadow because even though you don't want to kill her and even though you are a mother and understand why she did not run because you wouldn't have left your baby you know you cannot live with mother mouse though of course now that you have paid to put the soil under the porch you understand you have put a sign out: MICE WELCOME

and this poem recognizes that

so when you find yourself on the first day of fall which is not actually the first day but simply early October and because it has been such a dry hot summer the leaves aren't really turning so it looks enough like late spring to make you think back to when you and your sister used to catch the train from Cincinnati to Knoxville to go spend the summer with your grandparents and you thought you were pretty well grown because Mommy didn't have to travel with you and the two of you were given money which is not exactly true because your sister was given money and you were told to ask her if you wanted something and we couldn't wait to get to Jellico because the man came on the train with ham sandwiches which were made with butter instead of mayonnaise and ice cold little Cokes in a bottle and we had enough for that though we always shared the potato chips and we didn't have a care that the world was not a warm and welcoming place but we didn't realize that all up and down the line there was a congregation of Black men looking out for us that no one said or did anything to disturb our sense of well-being and what a loss that more Black men are in prison than on trains which don't exist protecting two little girls from the horrors of this world allowing them to grow up thinking people are kind so even though we lived in a segregated world and even though everybody knows that was wrong that band of brothers put their arms around us and got us from our mother to our grandmother seamlessly

and this poem recognizes that

and I do have a lawn jockey next to the river birch just a bit to the back of the birdbaths besides the bleached cow's head the ceramic elephant the rabbit and the talking dogs and you can easily see that I collect foolish things but they make me happy and I was ecstatic to see *Emerge* put Clarence Thomas the poster boy for lawn jockeys on the cover because I agree with the folk who say give Scalia two votes and save a salary since Thomas must surely be causing Thurgood Marshall many a turn-over in his grave while he talks about the disservice done to him by affirmative action though old Clarence didn't sell hurt until the nazi right was buying and I really don't understand how some people can take advantage of every affirmative initiative from college to law school to EEOC to the Supreme Court and say these programs do not work and even old foolish Shelby Steele was saying his children didn't need a scholarship as if the existence of the scholarship should be eliminated since he didn't and what kind of sense is that when you take a pitiful little dumbbunny like Armstrong Williams who says things like my parents taught me to work hard and behave myself as if other parents give lessons: *Now, Kwame, I want you to practice laziness today. You were far too busy yesterday* or worse: *Now, Kieshah, I expect loose morals from you. All last week you was studying and cleaning the house and helping out at the church and visiting the sick in the hospital and we just can't have none of that* and that is why those little lawn jockeys for the far right are so despicable because they lack not only good sense but common compassion and like the old jokes about Black people being just like a bunch of crabs the Black right is pulling people down because they think if they don't knock Black people down they will not be able to stay where they are and they are of course right because the only usefulness they have is to stand in opposition to progress and this poem recognizes that

so your back hurts anyway but you have to close things down as winter
will be here and no matter what else is wrong with winter the little lawn
jockeys get covered the mice find a home and little girls travel back and
forth with the love of Black men protecting them from the cold and even
when the Black men can't protect them they wish they could which has
to be respected since it's the best they can do and somehow you want to
pop popcorn and make pig feet and fried chicken and blueberry muffins
and some sort of baked apple and you will sit near your fire and tell tales
of growing up in segregated America and the tales will be so loving even
the white people will feel short-changed by being privileged and we call
it the blues with rhythm and they want it to be rock and roll and all the
thump thump thump coming from cars is not Black boys listening to rap
but all boys wishing they could be that beautiful boy who was a seed
planted in stone who grew to witness to the truth and who always kept it
real and lots of times there is nothing we can do through our pain and
through our tears but continue to love

and this poem recognizes that

The Poem for Frances Brown
(My First Warm Hearth Friend)

There are things you know . . . Clouds rise . . . Stars twinkle . . . Snow melts . . . Rain makes things grow . . . Sunshine warms . . . Trees cool . . .

If you love something . . . You will lose it

But the memory of motion . . . The wonder of the enchantment . . . The blue of the glacier . . . The blue of the sky . . . The blue in your heart . . . The reality of conclusion . . .

Though transforming . . . Stays

Yvonne and David

(A *Double Funeral on July 9, 1998*)

Of . . . they called her . . . bird . . . because they were taking French . . . and wanted to be cute . . . though I still don't see how they got "OF" from oiseau . . . She was very tall . . . over six feet . . . but before women played basketball . . . and before there was women's volleyball . . . and actually before women were supposed to do anything . . . except women things like cook . . . and clean . . . and sew . . . and take care of some man . . . when she could find him

Who knew the dreams . . . of too tall women . . . in too small villages . . . in too small towns . . . there really was no life . . . after high school . . . all there could be was some William Inge view . . . of the Midwest and the prince . . . but life was no picnic . . . and no one could wait to see . . . who might come along

But come along he did . . . nobody knows why now . . . I thought he was a dancer . . . the records show he was an architect . . . and an artist . . . and to Yvonne . . . a prince

Like out of some romantic novel . . . he stretched out his hand . . . and said Come with me . . . she was only nineteen . . . and her mother said No . . . but friends said Don't be a fool . . . plus he was drop-dead gorgeous . . . and with only the promise . . . of a great love for at least a little while . . . Of the bird . . . flew away

Small towns laugh because that's all they know how to do . . . thinking . . . maybe even hoping . . . it would not work . . . but work it did . . . and love they did . . . and a marriage . . . and a home . . . and dogs . . . and

forty years later . . . after college . . . her master's degree . . . her PhD . . .
they were still together

On a stormy night . . . when the dogs were at the groomer's and like dog
lovers everywhere . . . they were willing to brave the weather . . . to bring
the babies home . . . only there was this standing water . . . and this tree
. . . and that Rock Creek rising . . . and no way out of the car . . . and
David probably reached over to unhook her belt . . . as the car slid on its
side . . . and she got out but not up . . . and he was found in the car . . .
and she was found in the creek . . . and what began when she was nine-
teen ended when she was fifty-nine . . . and the only reason we can accept
it . . . is that they had lived happily together . . . and now they have died
together . . . and that's a sad story . . . but love is not always fun

For Just One Moment

I was not there
when Charlie Parker started playing between the notes
I could not be there
when Billie Holiday pondered the fruit of southern trees
I was unable to sit at a table
when Miles Davis gave birth to the Cool
but the musicians aren't the only ones who sing
and I am here with you
to hear my heart stop beating
for just one moment

This Poem

This poem is a worried poem . . . not rude but with a certain cryptic
attitude perhaps a certain roguish charm . . . a savoir faire that wants to
trouble the waters . . . it is on time though it broods . . . This poem has a
lot of questions and practically no answers . . . This poem wonders why

Sometimes this poem is very sad . . . it thinks about young Tupac Shakur
. . . there was trauma to the hands the death report showed . . . as if that
wonderful young man thought he could swat bullets . . . like Clinton
thought he could dodge Starr . . . like a topless dancer in a motorized
wheelchair thought she could do the shimmy

This worried poem thinks cancer is like a bad neighbor . . . not loud . . .
but messy . . . like the unchanging news when your son is dead . . . when
your father is dead . . . when your dreams are dying . . . like Michael Jor-
dan's father or Bill Cosby's son . . . just plain bad blues . . . when the news
won't change . . . This poem wants to be the seed planted in stone . . .
growing and climbing . . . no matter the lack of fertile soil and clean water
. . . thriving no matter the black-on-black crime . . . the white-on-white
crime . . . the white-on-black . . . no matter the news reports that never
change . . . never give the Black man his due . . . nor praise the Black
woman . . . just the same old news . . . which cannot change . . . when
your neighbor is like cancer . . . eating away . . . eating away . . . eating
away

This poem wants to be a conductor . . . on the new underground railroad
. . . wants to be the north star . . . leading the way . . . wants to be the moss
on the northern side of the tree . . . a bit of a surprise . . . something soft

in the night . . . This poem understands we cannot put a floor on poverty until we are willing to put a ceiling on wealth . . . if they are willing for us to define profits for business we will accept their definitions of freedom for humans

This poem wants to sing . . . jazz me baby, I'm blue . . . sometimes this poem points out Duke Ellington's "A Train" is to jazz what the "Star Spangled Banner" is to politics . . . an anthem we salute because of the power it represents . . . this poem remains curious: if Billie Holiday dies without children or husband why are her records still so expensive . . . but this poem knows the answer though we have to whisper it

This poem is new . . . like Athena slipping from Zeus' head . . . fully grown . . . all ready . . . able . . . anxious to play in Pandora's Box . . . laughing at the rest of us . . . struggling to survive . . . to thrive . . . to live a decent life . . . This poem admires the birds . . . the last dinosaurs on earth . . . and cries for the lions who are dying of tuberculosis

This poem dreams of sheets dried in the sun . . . pillows fluffed to their feathery height . . . quilts sewn by hand in intricate patterns . . . this poem dreams of home . . . while wishing it could step on the moon . . . or rocket to the sun . . . this poem is determined . . . to fight on

fugue

Me and Mrs. Robin

it's like you knew better than to get involved and you actually avoided any commitment to anything you can't actually control but then there was this thing in your chest and you knew even before your doctor said it that it was cancer and you really did not want to die yet it seemed so unfair somehow to say to the Gods well I don't want to die because most likely no one wants to die except a few people who are convinced that their pain and suffering cannot be eliminated without relinquishing their lives and Jack Kevorkian wants people to die with dignity but no one will stand up for our right to live in dignity and Jack is really crazy anyway because what most people need is drugs to relieve the pain but we live in a country that actually says to people with terminal diseases it is better to control the drugs lest you end up a junkie as if cancer patients live long enough to what? go out in the street and mug little old ladies? so for goodness sakes give me a break on that one but anyway I didn't want to be involved because once you make a commitment that is out of your control you are setting yourself up for a big hurt and everyone is hurt at some point and this thing which was set up to kill me was taken out by a kind and brilliant man and Gloria and Mike were on their way to Hawaii so they said: Stay at our home and get well and every day at the kitchen window there were the cardinals eating and doing that little trilling thing they do and every day I took drugs because I don't give a shit about the priorities of the American government and I smiled at the birds and felt better . . . you can see my problem

so when I came home I wanted to continue this relationship so we got a couple of feeders and for my morning activity I got up brushed my teeth showered and rested because it's incredible how tired you get when the up-per lobe of your left lung has been removed and even though Ginney said

I didn't have to come to the table I remembered all the old folk I knew who get up and get dressed and come to the table and I thought I should be at least as brave as they so instead of breakfast I had a sort of brunch but the reward for my getting up was that I could afternoon in the living room and watch the birds and they sang to me and I waved back so you can see it was only a matter of time

I would have thought I would have been better much sooner but I actually was not better and it was Spring and I was still brave and would shower and come to the table and I refused to be depressed because depression can kill you but I was still inside with not so much pain but a lot of fear of pain when a robin built a nest on the drain pipe and laid her eggs which I knew birds do but I didn't know that Father Robin brought food to Mother Robin and that he watched the nest while she took a break and that after Baby Robins were born he would come and feed them and she would feed them and they are very much like humans because they have their mouths open all the time unless they are asleep and they grew and you could see their little still heads as if they were not there which they were and then it was time for them to fly and that was just wonderful because the first one flew and he was a big bird and he strutted around on the front stoop and the second one flew and she was a bit more cautious but she got safely down and I was very proud and the third one just stood at the rim of the nest and cried and Mother Robin called and Brother and Sister Robin called but he cried and Mother Robin I would swear scolded him but he still wouldn't fly and finally I had to go to the bathroom which is exactly when I should not have because I guess he flew and when I didn't see him at the nest I was happy but then I noticed something on the ground and it was the little Robin who must have known something was wrong with him when he didn't want to fly but now he was on his side and I knew how scared he must be and how lonely he must be feeling and even though his mother was there offering blueberries from our blueberry bush you could see that he really felt he wasn't going to make it and for the first time in my life I was angry with God whom I had not questioned when my father had an intestinal cancer and had died nor when my first dog had a brain tumor and had to be relieved from her pain and I had not even questioned my own problem but had prayed that I could act like a civilized human being who well understands that life is not an infinite but only a possibility that we accept with grace and exercise in caution but this time with that scared hurt little Robin on the ground with the cats that are allowed to roam freely and kill a couple of million songbirds a year because their owners do not have to put a leash on them though if they were dogs their owners would have to take responsibility for them and not let them indiscriminately breed and leave little kittens to be run over by trucks and cars and people who think running over animals is fun so I cried which tends to be my solution to things that upset me and I did sort of holler at God: I hate you for this even though I know it's not God who does these things but Mother Nature and we are all lucky Mother Nature does not always get her way because she does not care about individuals but just the species and isn't that strange that we make the individual caring belong to God and Mother Nature indifferent to her children but I was angry because it seemed so unfair that before he had a chance at life there he was on the ground and maybe I was seeing a lot of people who have the same problem so I was standing at the window when Ginney came home and she said: What's the matter and I said God is killing that baby Robin and she went out to see what she could do but Mother and Father

Robin didn't know her so they put up a ruckus and attacked her and we decided to call our veterinarian who told us to call the wildlife folks who said they could save him if we could get him down to them in Roanoke so I went out because I thought the parents should know me and took a shoe box that we lined with an old cloth and I bent down while Ginney actually picked him up and even though I was crying I told her we wanted to save him and even though we knew we couldn't bring him back up the mountain because a wild bird will kill itself before we would be able to get home so I knew she was seeing her baby for the last time and I thought about how would I feel if I was seeing my son and I hoped she understood that I was just a human being doing the best that I could

so it's not hard to understand why I hate R. Kneck Kracker and Kracker's Pipe and Excavating Company who have destroyed the entire grove of trees who killed the nestlings who have confused the birds and murdered the possum and groundhogs because they want to build houses which could be built around trees with birds and possums and groundhogs and other things in mind but they come with their real live Tonka toys and cut a hill down to white boy size and they want someone to think they have done a job and they can't convince me that a job has to consist of killing things so I have no respect for the so-called developers or the so-called construction workers and the so-called Christiansburg City Council because the fires in Florida teach us that at some time in space even white people have to pay to the piper . . . and I hope it's a stiff price

Progress

i'm looking at old men . . . pregnant bellies hanging over worn blue jeans
. . . shirts open to expose old dried breasts were they on a woman . . . but
since they are on men just fatty useless tissue hanging . . . they are riding
yellow machines that shake my house . . . that scatter brittle white hairs
that the crows collect for nests . . . that smile stupid toothless smiles . . .
because they are once . . . again . . . called to rape the earth . . . though
they think of it as work . . . they stop to cool themselves in the shade of
my pine trees though if they had their way the trees would be ashes in
the wind since construction people always like to burn what they call
rubbish but what is actually warmth giving cool giving life giving green
. . . one wonders . . . why even so unbright a group as highway and byway
constructionists cannot find a way to save something that gives life while
they build something that most certainly will take life . . . they call it land
development as if somehow the green is undeveloped . . . the old men
stand and look and clank their balls together . . . as if some progress . . .
is being . . . made

In Which Case
(9-21-98)

like most people I am neither lazy nor so inclined to exertion that I would
be considered a pest yet . . . *r. kneck kracker* knocked on my door to say:
Your fence is five inches over my land . . . in which case I said: You're
wrong because I just had it surveyed in July . . . in which case he said:
You can see it yourself just go look . . . in which case I said: If I had
wanted to spot down fences I wouldn't have gone to college . . . in which
case he said: Well, it is . . . in which case I said: You owe me for your
water ruining my shed and drowning my magnolia tree and me having
to keep my house closed up while you try to make a swamp suitable for
building and speaking of my fence you have destroyed my gate . . . in
which case he said: I'm not going to argue with you . . . in which case I
said: Then why did you come . . . and he walked back to his black van-
type car thing not a Caravan but maybe a Chevy Suburban or whatever
low-riding house-type thing that you can commit crimes in and no one
can look through the windows to see which crime it is which was blocking
my driveway so that should I have chosen to flee my home in the face
of the threat of *kneck* banging on my front door causing my dog to bark
furiously though she is a very small dog and could not cause harm other
than alarm I would have been unable to do so . . . in which case I called
my lawyer to ask what can I do to protect myself from *kneck* and my
fence from his yellow machines which already have killed my bushes
because he came too close to my line and now I can't sleep because he
is a known bully who does his work in the cover of night and somehow
it does not make sense to me that *mr. way* is a concrete plant owner and
I rejoiced when he resigned from city council but the kicker on pick five
or the icing on the cake or actually adding insult to injury is *way's* state-
ment that: **all land zoned agriculture should be rezoned development**

and guess which materials should be used and is it me or is something very wrong with fat old corrupt white men on their last legs but determined to take everything down with them so council created a very special seat for *way* on the planning commission and if there is no moderation it is because they show no sense and if there is hatred it is because they constantly threaten and when there are reactions people will say let's seek reconciliation and what we really seek is their heads on some sort of stakes so that pigeons can have a target to shit on and like most people I am not so lazy as to not understand what's wrong nor so energetic that I seek change but I just started out wanting a home with a few birds a television with cable and some peace and quiet and this old fat bastard of a robber baron has no right coming to my home saying anything to me about anything that's what his lawyer and my lawyer are supposed to talk about so I assume he is threatening me for some other reason . . . in which case I cannot protect myself but I can acknowledge it is a threat

Writing Lessons

There are . . . still . . . so many books I want to read . . . and reread . . .

There are . . . still . . . so many places I want to travel . . . to . . .

There are . . . still . . . foods I want to eat . . . and drinks I want to sample . . .

There are . . . blankets to lie upon or under . . .

There are . . . pillows upon which to prop my books or my head . . .

I definitely want to rocket to outer space . . . I also want to explore inner space . . .

I know no one ever wished they had been meaner . . .

Or hated more . . .

Or spent more hours away from people they loved . . .

I know that life is interesting and you can never go wrong Being interested

If I were giving advice I would say: Sing
   People who sing to themselves
   People who make variations on songs they know
   People who teach songs to other people
   These are the people other people want to be with

and that will let you be a good writer
   Because

There are . . . still . . . so many ideas to conceive

Iverson's Posse

Here is a free piece of advice which you know what it is worth because you know what you paid for it: Send your posse to school

They say they love you and are your friend but what have they done for you lately

It's not that you need the car you can buy another car and another and another until your knees give out or your back gives out or you land on the wrong side of your foot and your ankle gives out but none of these things will happen Allen because you are young and talented and beautiful so if they love you they should show it isn't that what you tell the girls but baby how do I know unless you show me

So let them show you

OK OK you say they are not all that smart and what good will school do them and frankly son I don't know ... maybe they are dumb and maybe school cannot do anything for them but school can do something for you because you don't seem to trust anyone but your posse and you don't seem to want to be with anyone but them and maybe you're scared of them maybe you think if you find new friends they will just shoot you down or rape your mother or whatever it is that men do to each other when they are afraid of being left behind I know what they do to women so maybe it's the same thing but they say you are their friend and you have proven you are their friend but what have they proven to you

Send your posse to school

If they are out of high school send them to college and please don't tell me they can't go to college because even I know many many colleges who will take anyone even your posse and the money you will save sending the three of them to school will be immediately realized and what is more you will get a posse who can offer you some real protection

Have one of them major in pre-law so that you can get the proper representation you need when the other folks start coming at you and when your team tries to trade you and they don't want to honor your contract and they find some crazy Black woman or crazier white one to say you have raped her or looked at her like you wanted to and you have embarrassed our team for the last time and things of that nature you will have your own friend to represent your best interest and not be like poor Mike Tyson who gets screwed by everyone because he didn't have a posse to help him out though he did have Tupac but they murdered him

Have one of them major in accounting or finance or business and please don't tell me they can't major in mathematical-based studies because anyone who can measure milligrams of things and anyone who can figure out how much water with how much powder and anyone who can flip a wad of bills and tell if it is short or not can do the math and they need to do the math for you instead of against themselves and certainly you need to Have one

Major in religion so that one will be able to go anywhere at anytime park anywhere and hear everything and still be able to testify to your good nature and how much you are beloved by the Beings who look after us

And someone will say How silly those boys don't need to go to school but they do Iverson because right now they are little more than domesticated dogs who sit around waiting for you to bring your light and no one should be in the dark because someone else is out working so send your posse to school

It's the right thing to do

Mrs. Bat

maybe it was because it was hot
maybe it was too many gnats
maybe the moon didn't come
or the stars didn't glow
maybe something frightened the group
winging home after a night's full meal
but one little bat like E.T. got left behind
and when daylight came had to hide herself
she chose the tennis court where I play
and when I looked at the baby bat
she shut her eyes real tight
she turned and turned as if I wouldn't notice
that she is alive and scared
we decided to play on another court
and accidentally locked everything up
the next morning she was gone
no note no thank yous just gone
but I'm a mother too
and I would expect no less of mrs. bat
than she expects of me

Clouds

I want to swim with hippos
jump with salmon
fly with geese
land with robins
walk with turtles
sleep with possum
dress with penguins
preen with peacocks
fish with grizzlies
hunt with lions
forage with pigs for truffles
eat nuts with the squirrels
plant seeds with the wind
and ride on off with the clouds
at the end

SEEDS
(FOR JEAN PATRICE)

EVEN SEEDS CAN MAKE A COVER . . . NOT ONLY LEAVES
AND BRANCHES

EVEN SEEDS CAN RIDE SPRING WINDS . . . NOT ONLY
SPORES AND DANDELION THINGS

SEEDS ESPECIALLY SPREAD THE GOOD NEWS: A TREE . . . A
BUSH . . . A FLOWER IS COMING

ONE NOTE SEEDS A SONG . . . ONE PENNY SEEDS A SAVINGS
ONE HOPE SEEDS A LIFE

AND JEAN PATRICE IS THE SEED WHO FULFILLS THE
HOPES OF CHILDREN AND ADULTS . . . WHO SEEDS THE
DREAMS OF A FAIRER WORLD . . . WHO IS THE SEED OF
THIS EARTH IN THE WARMTH OF OUR HEARTS

Sunday

hot rolls in a summer basket
fried chicken piled on the platter
lemons squeezed for lemonade
blackberries sugared for pudding
corn on the cob is steaming in butter
green beans surrounding a ham hock
salt and pepper and hot sauce too
    after all it's Sunday

The Things We Love About Winter

There is popcorn
and steamed oysters
and cauliflower soup
and beaten biscuits
and even blackberry cobbler
and fried apples
and hard-boiled eggs
and the juiciest oranges
and homemade cards with Elmer's glue holding ribbons and pictures down
and a beautiful roast turkey stuffed with giblets
and sage
and pecan pieces
and everybody is happy because it's Christmas
and now we can cuddle up for a long winter's nap
and make believe it is Spring

On My Journey Now

There is this special feeling you get
when you snuggle under a quilt
that was made by your great-grandmother,
washed and cared for by your mother
passed on to you soft clean sweet smelling from the days before
washing machines did wash
and dry cleaners did pressing

There is this special feeling you get
when you remember the smell of fat meat boiling
in the pot waiting for the greens to come and share a smaller space

There is a feeling you get
when you look back at the beauty and wonder of our people
that sends apple boiling smells
to tickle your nose
that lets you know "Yes" this is not my home
only my STOP on a journey   And one day you know you'll take
the next step to that glorious plane

A Blackbird on My Knee

I'm Windex without a window   Drano without the sludge
I'm wax without hardwood   Mean without a grudge
I'm a poem without rhyme   A clock without time
A rabbit on crutches   A meat-eating deer
Without you around one thing is clear

I'm horse with no kick   A bee with no sting
My hair won't plait   My bell can't ring
I'm a quilt without filling   I take without stealing
I'm savings without interest   Stocks without bonds
My goldfish have moved to my neighbor's ponds

I sing to no music
I rap to no beat
My heart is too heavy   I need a retreat

I'm lonely and weary   I can't get rest
I'm unsatisfied since I've had the best
You need to come home and take care of me
I said you need to come home and take care of me
I'm just sitting in this vacant lot with a blackbird on my knee

The Little Choo Choo Train

Johnny got a choo choo
Sarah took the plane
Johnny kept that choo choo
So he could come again
Rode it to the circus
Rode it to the store
Fell out of the Ferris wheel
It hurt him to the core
Sarah went to New York
Saw Fifth Avenue
Looked at Johnny broken down
Said we are too through

Convenient Haystacks

The ostrich talked and the goldfish walked while the little dog
wagged its tail

The lion roared the rhino bored a black hole through the jail

The elephant laughed to see such a sight the hyenas howled through
it all

The moon shined down on the prairie dog town while you and I
danced at the ball the ball
while you and I danced at the ball

And though it was great we really were late getting the carriage back

So off we walked to talk sweet talk making stops by convenient
haystacks haystacks
making stops by convenient haystacks

Lasso the Sun

Lasso the sun then
turn it around
it's time for the night to begin

Turn out the light
speckle the clouds
haul out the moon for its smile

A bevy of bats
to crackle the air
the possum family goes walking

My cat meows
the dog bow wows
an autumn breeze whispers the gossip

Kiss a Frog
(A Lullaby)

write a letter write a song
tell a story right or wrong
kiss a frog and make a prince
mix the sugar with the quince
eight and forty in a pie that is   hummingbirds
what a lie
light the candle see the bear
west winds blowing time to care
for the babies sleeping tight
through the sweet dreams of the night

The Rain

Spring rains are my favorite
they help the flowers grow
Winter rain makes good ice cream
because it's really snow

Traveling seeds ride windy rains
Thirsty trees scrape windowpanes

Autumn rains make all leaves change
from green to burnished reds
Soft rains wash our tears away
and rainbows warm our beds

One Stops on My Windowpane

dandelions get blown away and ride the kite winds to the trees
surfing on their rainbow dreams
one stops on my windowpane

sunflower heads get pulled away he loves me not he loves me
yellow petals sky the breeze
one stops on my windowpane

small black flies buzz round the ice cream where it melted down
shoo shoo flies they fly away
then they turn and pirouette
one stops on my windowpane

shoo shoo shoo kabang

Brought 2 U by . . .

Violet

Verbally
Vocalizes
Valiantly
Validly
Vehemently
Valorously
Vastly
Vitriolically
Vividly
Voluntarily
Vulnerably
Vainly
Vainly
Vainly
Not
Victoriously
Against
Violence

Brought 2 U by the Letter V

The Last Poem

The Last Poem on the last day will be a love poem . . . maybe not passionate . . . certainly not sexy . . . maybe even a bit on the boring side . . . most likely tedious . . . perhaps a bit . . . overbearing . . . probably too protective . . . but a love poem . . . nonetheless

The Last Poem will not swing from trees . . . will never find Jane and boy . . . is King of Nothing

The Last Poem on the last day will not shoot turtles in the head to play pranks on fraternity boys . . . will not take repeating rifles to prairie dog towns to see how high a little rodent will go when splayed by a 30.06 . . . the last poem will not speed by in a motor boat grazing a manatee which will then develop an infection . . . and die. No. The Last Poem will not hunt down the white tigers or wipe out an entire elephant community just to get one baby elephant for some crazy circus . . . neither will The Last Poem have Indonesian children making Nikes they can't afford to buy to sell to Black children who can't afford to buy either . . . The Last Poem will not be mean . . . or murderous

The Last Poem on the last day will . . . however . . . scream

The Last Poem will weep the eternal scream of one who has seen a mother robin go off to hunt worms for the nestlings to come back to a mountain of dirt . . . because **Kracker's Pipe and Excavating Company** works for R. Kneck Kracker who wants to bring a small hill down to a smaller size and the fact that other living beings have a home in a small hill has no credit in his bank. The bird left her nestlings expecting to return to them and . . . returning to a tree that had been upended and covered with dirt tried to peck her way into the dirt. The Last Poem on the first day hates R. Kneck Kracker and Kracker's Pipe and Excavating Company and City Council of Christiansburg, Virginia, for being assholes . . . for killing birds and possums and groundhogs . . . for being greedy human beings who continually give humans a bad name to other living things. The Last Poem on the first day hopes it survives just long enough to say I told you so but since no one listens and since some crazy-greedy-belly-hanging-over-face-lifted white people never ever get the connection between the evil they do and the hatred they cause maybe The Last Poem should just weep and maybe The Last Poem should just get a glass of wine and maybe after The Last Poem decides it is The Last Poem maybe it will build a meadow and feed the birds and pray for lightning to strike down destroyers who call themselves construction workers . . . sort of politicians who are called statesmen and police who are called peace officers and judges who are called learned

The Last Poem is sick and tired of the barely intelligent . . . barely sane . . . totally greedy . . . running the world

The Last Poem on the last day may simply hang its head . . . and walk away . . . and the Republicans will say poems were never needed . . . anyway

so The Last Poem on the very last day in an act of love and humility . . . will go bang bang bang . . . to try to make it right